Fish in the Sea from A to Z

By Soren Pilman

For my grandchildren

Angelfish

Bb

Barracuda

Cc

Clownfish

Also called Anemonefish

Dorado

Also called Mahi-mahi and Dolphinfish

Ee

Eagle Ray

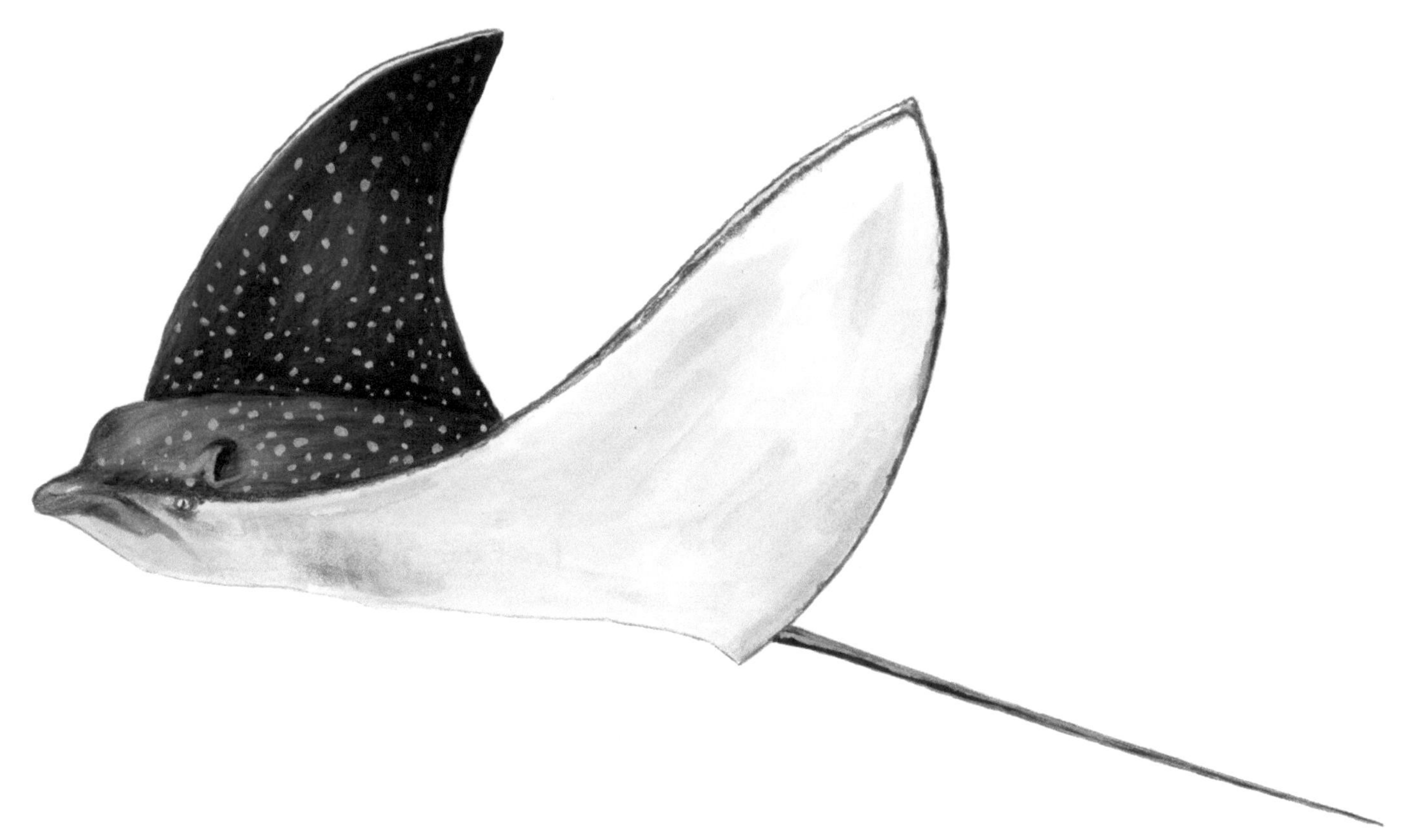

Ff

Frogfish

Gar

Hammerhead
Shark

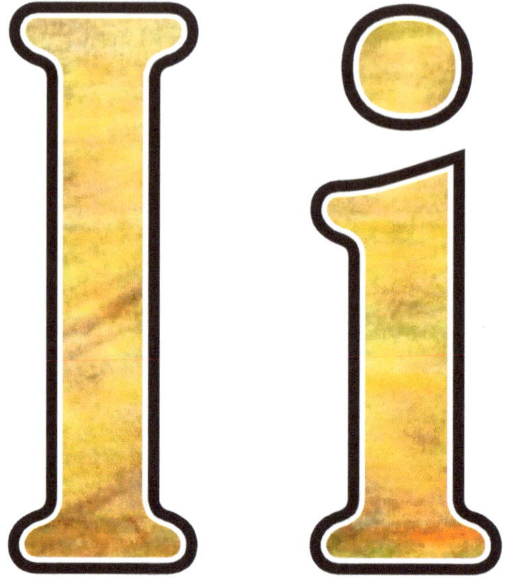

Inanga

John Dory

Also called St. Peter's fish

Kk

Koi

Ll

Largemouth
Bass

Marlin

Northern Pike

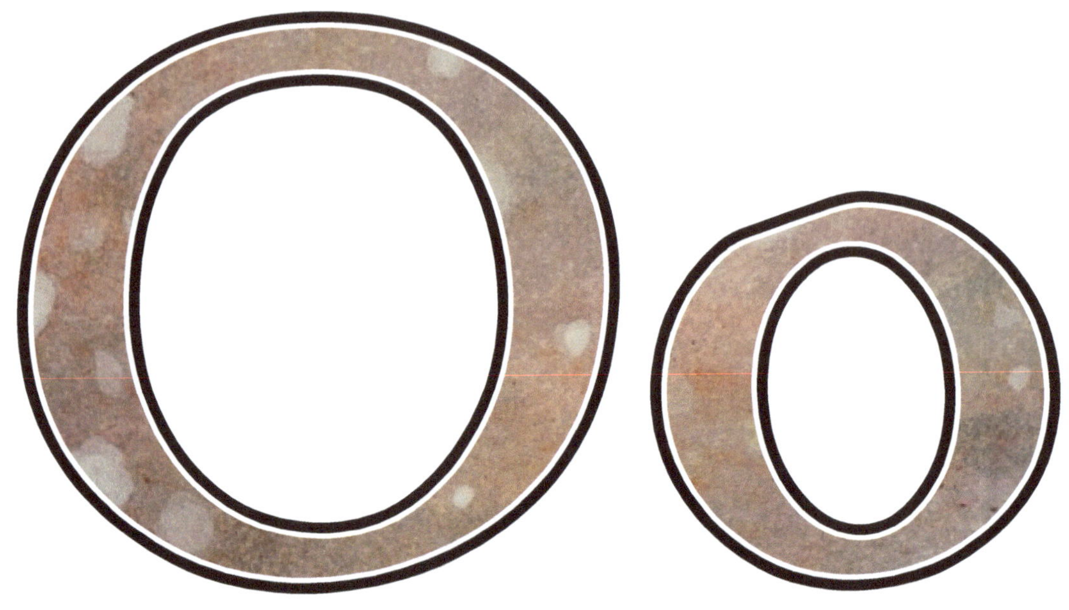

Opah

Also called Moonfish

Piranha

Quillback
Rockfish

Ridgehead

Sturgeon

Tuna

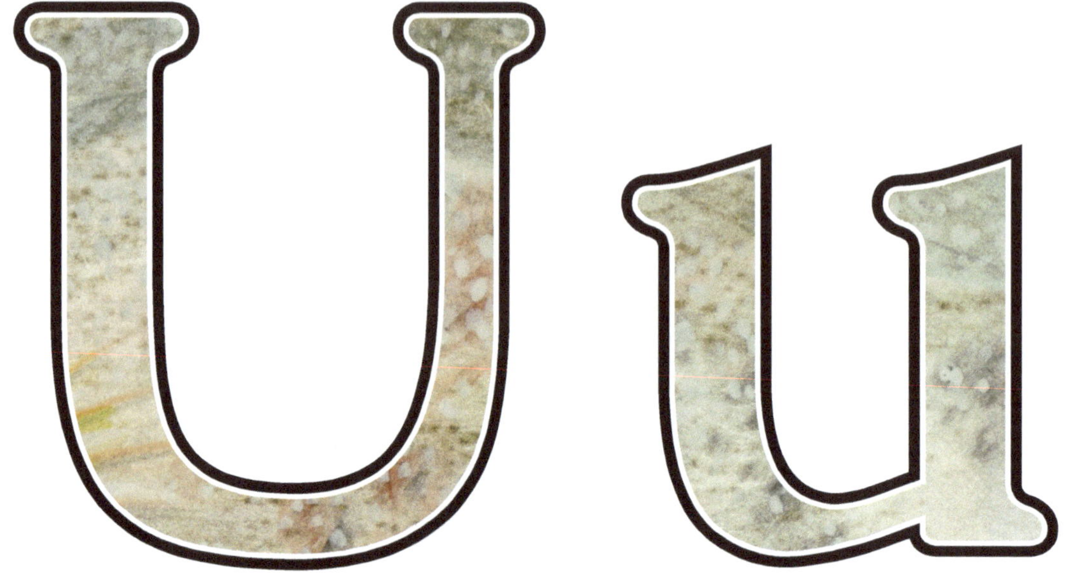

Uaru

Ventrifossa

Walleye

Xx

X-Ray Tetra

Yellow Tang

Zebra Tilapia

www.ingramcontent.com/pod-product-compliance
Lightning Source LLC
Chambersburg PA
CBHW040138240726
48664CB00002B/522